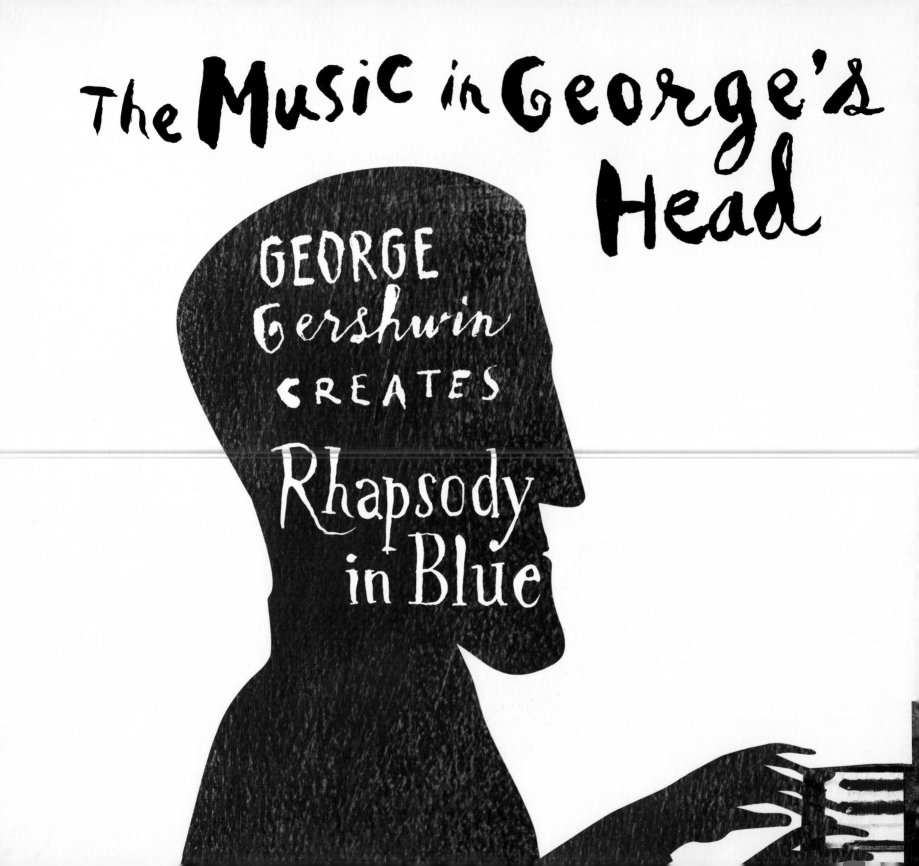

The Music in George's Head

GEORGE Gershwin CREATES

Rhapsody in Blue

Suzanne Slade

Illustrated by Stacy Innerst

CALKINS CREEK
AN IMPRINT OF HIGHLIGHTS
Honesdale, Pennsylvania

With love to Freddie, Julie,
Nick, and Aaron
—SS

For my mother and father,
who allowed us to make a lot of noise—
and music
—SI

I frequently hear MUSIC in the very heart of Noise.

—George Gershwin

George heard music all the time.
At home. At school.
Even when he was roller-skating down New York's busy streets.

Sometimes he was so busy listening to the beautiful music in his head,
he didn't pay attention to other things—like getting to school on time.

Now, George wasn't a troublemaker. He just couldn't stop thinking

about *Melody in F,*

a *classical* tune he'd heard at the penny arcade.

No one knew George was interested in music until his mother
decided the family needed a piano. George's older brother, Ira, took one
look at the secondhand instrument and headed to his room. But George
ran to the piano, spun the stool down, and lifted the keyboard cover.
When he felt those smooth keys beneath his fingers, his face lit up like
the lights on Broadway.

Without a word, he pounded out a popular RAGTIME tune.

His mother was amazed! She had no idea he'd been practicing on a friend's player piano.

George began studying with some of the best piano teachers in town. At night he sneaked into concerts to hear famous pianists play. He pasted pictures of his favorite composers—Liszt, Ornstein, and Busoni— into his music scrapbook.

When he was fifteen, George started working at Remick's
music store. He played sheet music that customers asked to hear.

George also wrote his own tunes —
lively, FUN, and DIFFERENT.

At seventeen, he sold his first one.

Three years later, on a bumpy bus ride, George heard

New Melodies

among the clatter and noise of New York's bustling streets.

Toes tapping, he plucked out notes for a tune called "Swanee."
The loud music annoyed his father, but George kept on playing.
He just couldn't quit thinking about those city noises.

Millions of people bought recordings of "Swanee." Soon
George was invited to every party in town, where he played
biddly-bop

BLUES tunes all night long. By 1920
everyone knew George Gershwin, the young hit songwriter.

People wondered what kind of music the bold, creative composer would write next. But George already knew— **JAZZ**.

As a boy, he roller-skated to New York's Harlem neighborhood to hear the smooth, syncopated jazz rhythms in clubs and restaurants. Most "serious" musicians thought jazz wasn't music at all. *The notes were RESTLESS, Untamed.*

The rhythms were WILD.

Unpredictable.

Bandleader Paul Whiteman loved George's WILD, RESTLESS music.
Determined to prove hip musicians like George were playing important music,
Whiteman planned a concert—"An Experiment in Modern Music."
He was sure people would go crazy for this

new JAZZY razzmatazz.

George set out to compose a dazzling, daring piece for the concert. One that showed jazz was exciting, Limitless. FREE.

He scratched his head

and paced the floors – and scratched and paced some more.

and paced

He'd barely written a single note when he had to leave town for the opening of his new musical, Sweet Little Devil.

The train's steely wheels creaked into motion.

Rattle·ty·BANG!

Its huge wheels rolled faster and faster.

Rattle·ty·BANG! Rattle·ty·BANG!

Faster still, the heavy wheels seemed to fly over the metal track.

Rattle·ty·BANG! Rattle·ty·BANG! Rattle·ty·BANG!

And that's when George heard it—music!

Notes. Rhythms. Slow and steady. Fast and furious.

The train noises created New Melodies in his head. He thought about

the old, familiar music he loved—classical, Ragtime, JAZZ, and the BLUES.

The different styles of music blended together into one beautiful rhapsody.

George heard his concerto. He even saw the notes on paper!

Back home, George finished his concerto. It was just
as he'd planned—

daring, and razzmatazz dazzling!

It was a musical kaleidoscope of America's melting pot—

Rhapsody in Blue.

Duke Ellington

With the concert only one week away, George and the orchestra started practicing.

During rehearsal, a clarinet player decided to play a joke on George. At the beginning of the rhapsody, his clarinet let out a long, whooping wail: *WuaaaAAAAAAAAAAAAAAAA!*

All the musicians laughed.

But George didn't.

He told the clarinet player to wail like that in the concert.

A silent, silvery snow decorated
the city for the big day, February 12, 1924.
Hurried feet pounded

staccato beats

as people rushed inside Aeolian Hall.

Every seat was filled.

The lights dimmed.

The first of the twenty-six musical numbers began.

Backstage, George listened.

And waited.

He was scheduled to perform next to last.

As the band *blew, plucked, and strummed,*
the packed hall grew hot and stuffy. Eyelids began to close.
People squirmed in their seats. Some stood up to leave.

Then George sat down at the piano.

A clarinet fluttered softly, like butterfly wings on a morning breeze.

George smiled at the clarinet player.

AAAAAAAAAAAA! the clarinet wailed as it slid up eighteen notes.

Sleepy eyes flew open. Restless listeners sat still.

People heading for the door hurried back to their seats.

Trombones and trumpets blew brassy sounds—small and soft,
then big and bright.

Velvety violins started to sing.

More musicians joined in. Each carefully playing
their sheets of music.

Fingers flying, George made those piano keys

MARCH. SKIP. Dance.

But he didn't have sheet music.

George played
        the notes in his head.

The room was electrified. Energized.
People were surprised to hear
New Melodies

mixed with classical,
Ragtime, Jazz, and the Blues.

George's Rhapsody in Blue

was smooth and sultry.
Brash and bouncy!
It turned into an up-tempo march melody.

No one had ever heard anything like it.
Except George.
He'd been hearing beautiful music all his life.

It was on the train, with its steely rhythms, its rattle-ty-bang that is often so stimulating to a composer....And there I suddenly heard—and even saw on paper—the complete construction of the rhapsody, from beginning to end.

—George Gershwin

Author's Note

George Gershwin composed a long list of tunes during his short thirty-eight-year life. This story presents significant events in George's life that illustrate his connection to various kinds of music that appear in *Rhapsody in Blue.*

At the young age of six, George fell in love with classical music. He later shared his memories of that momentous day: "I stood outside a penny arcade listening to an automatic piano leaping through [Anton] Rubinstein's *Melody in F.* The peculiar jumps in the music held me rooted. To this very day I can't hear the tune without picturing myself outside that arcade on One Hundred and Twenty-fifth Street, standing there barefoot and in overalls, drinking it all in avidly."

When the Gershwins' first piano arrived in 1910, everyone assumed Ira, the good student and oldest child, would become the family pianist. Although he'd taken lessons from his aunt, Ira had no interest in playing piano. But as soon as the piano arrived, George masterfully played a popular ragtime tune. He later confessed he'd learned to play by following the keys on a friend's player piano and by secretly playing at the local piano store where he ran errands.

As a boy, George enjoyed stickball, street hockey, and roller-skating. But he loved music more, so he skated to fancy restaurants and clubs in the Harlem neighborhood, where jazz bands played. Mesmerized by the lively, exciting beat, he often sat outside the clubs for hours, skates still strapped to his feet!

George said, "I frequently hear music in the very heart of noise." This proved true when he and his friend Irving Caesar hopped a bus to the Gershwins' apartment in 1919. During the ride, city noises inspired one of his first hits, "Swanee." While George worked out the notes, Irving wrote the lyrics to go with the song. Although George's father was annoyed when their music disrupted his poker game, he later played along with a tissue-covered comb.

After a famous performer named Al Jolson started singing "Swanee," it quickly became the most popular song in America. As George's fame skyrocketed, he received invitations to parties all over town. George enjoyed talking to new people at parties, but he was happiest when he was at a keyboard playing tunes for guests.

Through the years, many new melodies and musical themes popped into George's head. At age twenty, he began writing these tunes in diaries so he wouldn't forget them. Some of his ideas were only a few notes. Others were complete melodies. When George started composing new pieces, he often used his music diaries for inspiration.

Music from George's life—classical, ragtime, jazz, blue notes—and a "rattle-ty-bang" train—inspired *Rhapsody in Blue*. But this piece also contains other musical influences. For example, the opening clarinet wail (which began as a joke) is reminiscent of the klezmer music George heard at bar mitzvahs, weddings, and other Jewish celebrations.

In 1924 George and Ira decided to create new songs together. George composed the tunes, while Ira wrote the perfect lyrics to go with them. This legendary team produced hundreds of songs for Hollywood and Broadway, including "I Got Rhythm," "Someone to Watch Over Me," and "Embraceable You." They wrote everything from musicals such as *Lady, Be Good!* to their acclaimed opera, *Porgy and Bess*. Known for his unique musical style, George used

real taxicab horns in his score *An American in Paris* to share the sounds of the French city with his audience.

George's musical talents were cut short when he died from a brain tumor at age thirty-eight. But he will never be forgotten. In 1985 George and Ira were awarded the Congressional Gold Medal for their musical achievements. The George and Ira Gershwin Room opened in the Library of Congress in 1998. Every year, thousands of people visit this exhibit to remember George and the beautiful music he created. The Library of Congress Gershwin Prize for Popular Song is awarded to outstanding artists who, like George, have devoted their lives and careers to music.

Illustrator's Note

The depictions of the clothing, architecture, and transportation are based on archival photographs. The musicians shown at the February 12, 1924 concert are an amalgamation of the many musicians and influences in George Gershwin's musical life.

Timeline

1898 Jacob Gershvin is born on September 26, although everyone calls him "George."

The Gershvin family later changes their last name to *Gershwin*.

1904 In a penny arcade, George hears an automatic piano playing *Melody in F*.

1910 The Gershwins buy a wooden upright piano. George begins taking piano lessons.

George starts a scrapbook with programs from concerts he attended.

1914 World War I begins.

George becomes a "song plugger," playing songs for customers at Remick's music store in Tin Pan Alley (a neighborhood where music publishers and songwriters worked).

1918 World War I ends.

1919 October—George composes the music for "Swanee" and his friend Irving Caesar writes the lyrics.

1920 "Swanee" recording sung by Al Jolson sells millions of copies.

1924 George takes a train to Boston for the premiere of his musical, *Sweet Little Devil*.

February 12—*Rhapsody in Blue* makes its debut at "An Experiment in Modern Music" concert in Aeolian Hall, which is packed with music lovers, critics, and important musicians such as Sergei Rachmaninoff and John Philip Sousa.

December 1—George and Ira's first musical collaboration, *Lady, Be Good!*, opens on Broadway. George wrote the music and Ira wrote the lyrics.

1927 The first feature-length movie with talking and music, *The Jazz Singer*, is released.

1928 George composes *An American in Paris* to share his experiences in the French capital.

1929 The Great Depression begins.

1931 George composes *Second Rhapsody*, which incorporates a flyswatter.

1935 George completes his opera, *Porgy and Bess*.

1937 At age thirty-eight, George dies from a brain tumor.

Selected Bibliography*

All quotations used in the book can be found in the following source marked with a double asterisk (**).

Cowen, Ron. "George Gershwin: He Got Rhythm." *Washington Post*, 1998. washingtonpost.com/wp-srv/national/horizon/nov98/gershwin.htm.

Feinstein, Michael. *The Gershwins and Me: A Personal History in Twelve Songs*. With Ian Jackman. New York: Simon & Schuster, 2012.

**Goldberg, Isaac. *George Gershwin: A Study in American Music*. New York: Frederick Ungar Publishing, 1958. (Some experts consider this biography a primary source as it was written with George's cooperation and complete approval.)

Hyland, William G. *George Gershwin: A New Biography*. Westport, CT: Praeger Publishers, 2003.

Library of Congress, George and Ira Gershwin Collection. rs5.loc.gov/service/music/eadxmlmusic/eadpdfmusic/2010/mu010014.pdf.

Perlis, Vivian, and Libby Van Cleve. *Composers' Voices from Ives to Ellington: An Oral History of American Music*. New Haven, CT: Yale University Press, 2005.

Pollack, Howard. *George Gershwin: His Life and Work*. Berkeley: University of California Press, 2006.

Rayno, Don. "Gershwin by Grofé." Harmonie Ensemble New York. harmonieensembleny.com/pdf/gershwin-grofe-notes.pdf.

Schwartz, Charles. *Gershwin: His Life and Music*. Indianapolis: Bobbs-Merrill, 1973.

"The Gershwin Brothers." Gershwin.com. gershwin.com/the-gershwin-brothers.

E-mail Correspondence with Author

Michael E. Ruhling, PhD, professor of performing arts, Rochester Institute of Technology, and president of the Haydn Society of North America, 2012–15.

Raymond A. White, music specialist, George and Ira Gershwin Collection, Library of Congress, Washington, D.C., 2012–15.

*Websites active at time of publication

Acknowledgments

With gratitude to Raymond A. White, music specialist, George and Ira Gershwin Collection, Library of Congress; and Michael E. Ruhling, PhD, professor of performing arts, Rochester Institute of Technology, and president of the Haydn Society of North America, for sharing their expertise on this project.

—SS

Text copyright © 2016 by Suzanne Slade
Illustrations copyright © 2016 by Stacy Innerst
All rights reserved.

For information about permission to reproduce selections from this book, please contact permissions@highlights.com.

Calkins Creek
An Imprint of Highlights
815 Church Street
Honesdale, Pennsylvania 18431
Printed in China

ISBN: 978-1-62979-099-2
Library of Congress Control Number: 2015958417

First edition

10 9 8 7 6 5 4 3 2 1

Designed by Barbara Grzeslo
Production by Sue Cole
Text set in Kabel LT Std
About the illustrations and hand lettering: The illustrations were done in acrylic on paper. Scanned textiles and papers were also incorporated.

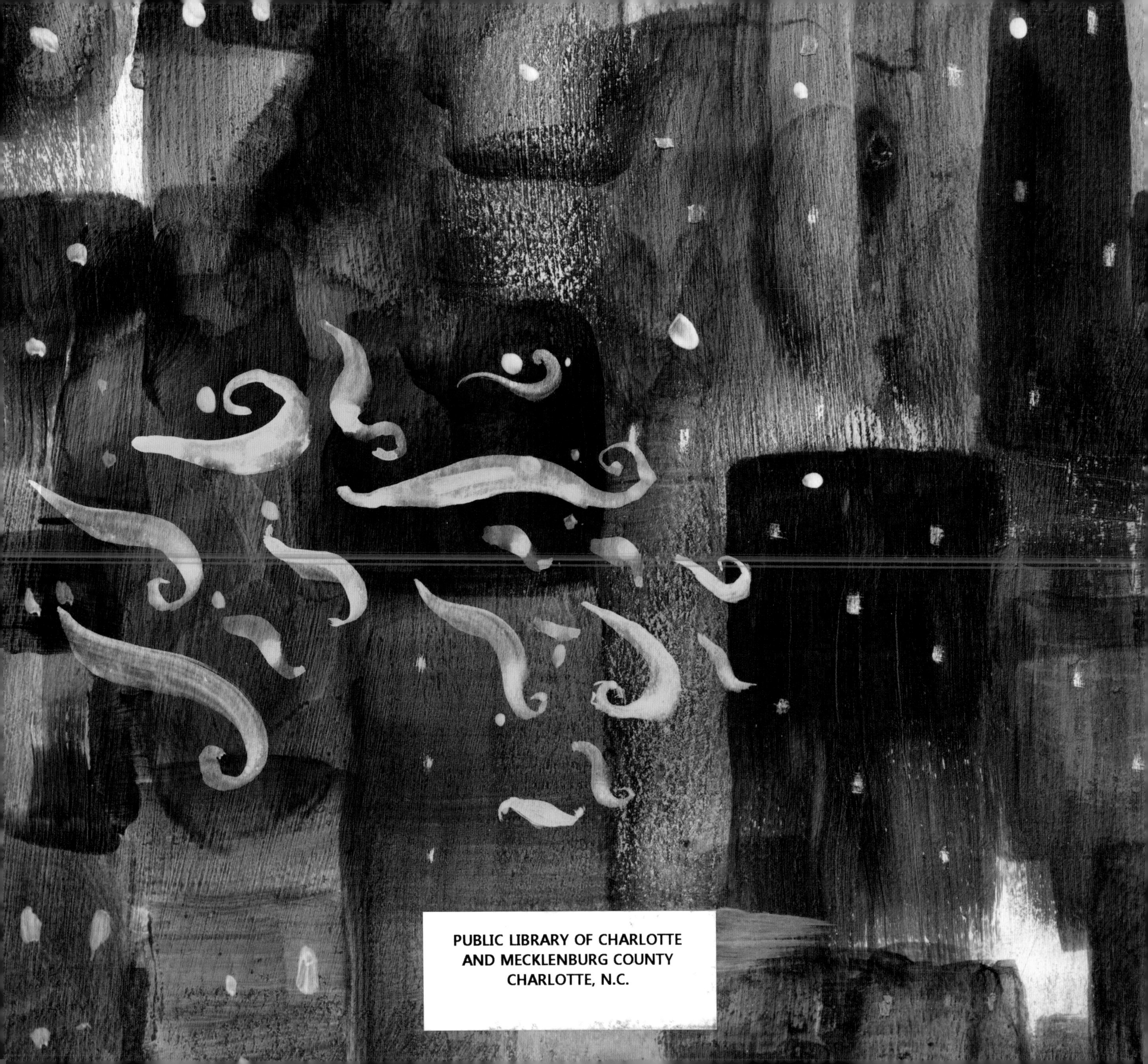